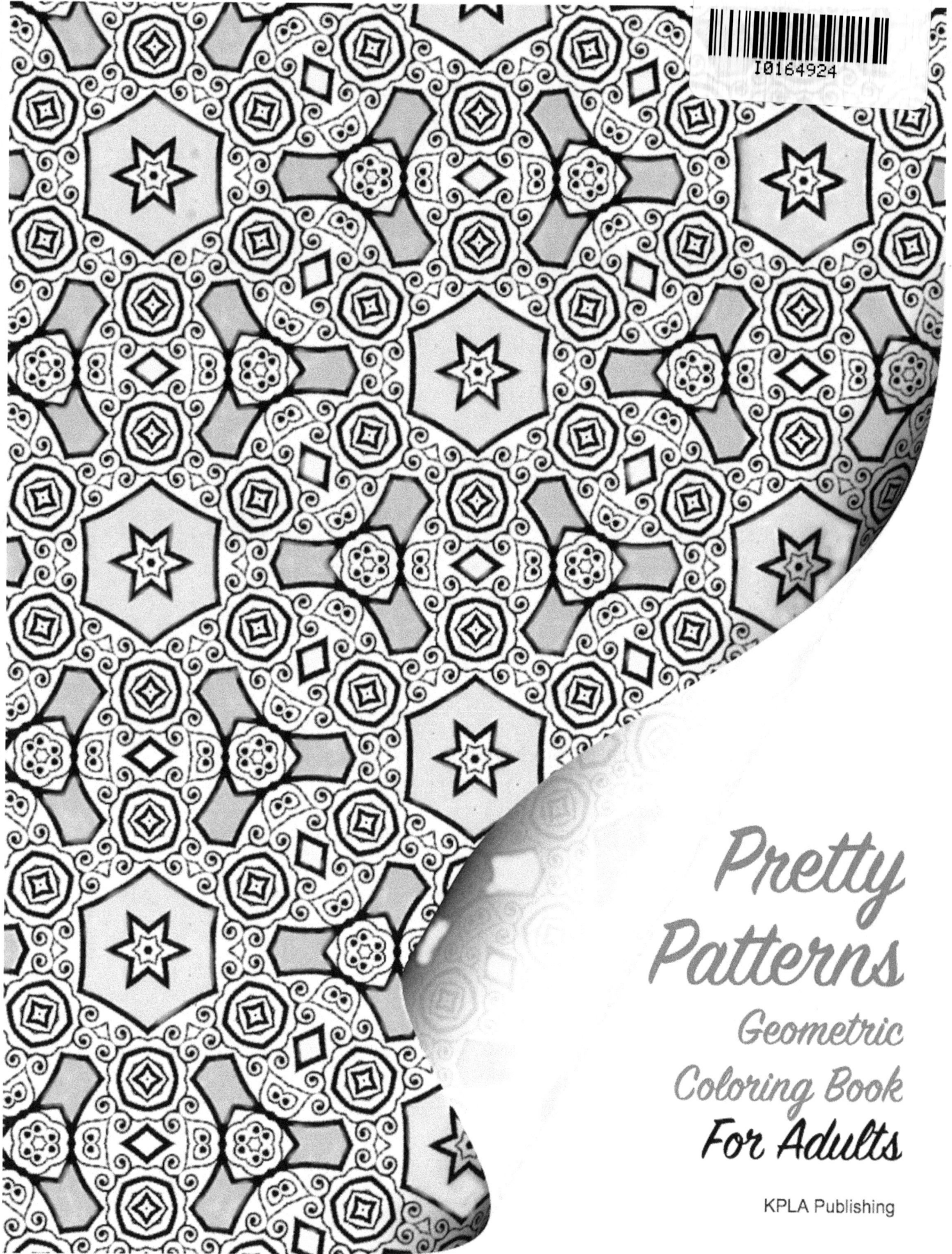

Pretty Patterns

Geometric

Coloring Book

For Adults

KPLA Publishing

Pretty Patterns Geometric Coloring Book for Adults
ISBN 13 – 978-1-943833-15-3
ISBN 10 - 1-943833-15-X
Copyright 2017 © by KPLA Publishing; designed by Kimberly Millionaire

Published by:
KPLA Publishing – Kissed Publications
PO Box 9819
Hampton, VA 23670
www.kplapublishing.com

10 9 8 7 6 5 4 3 2 1

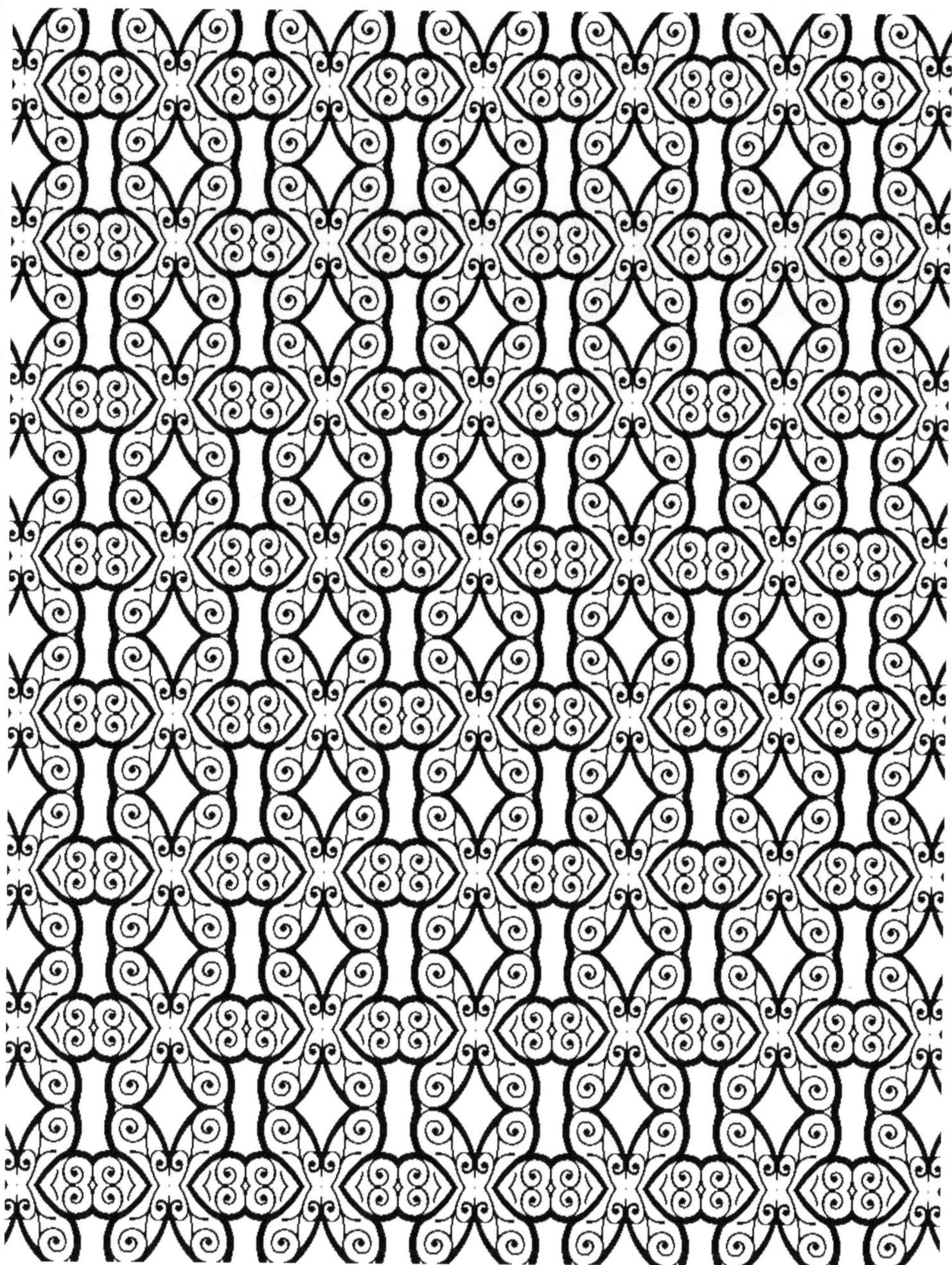

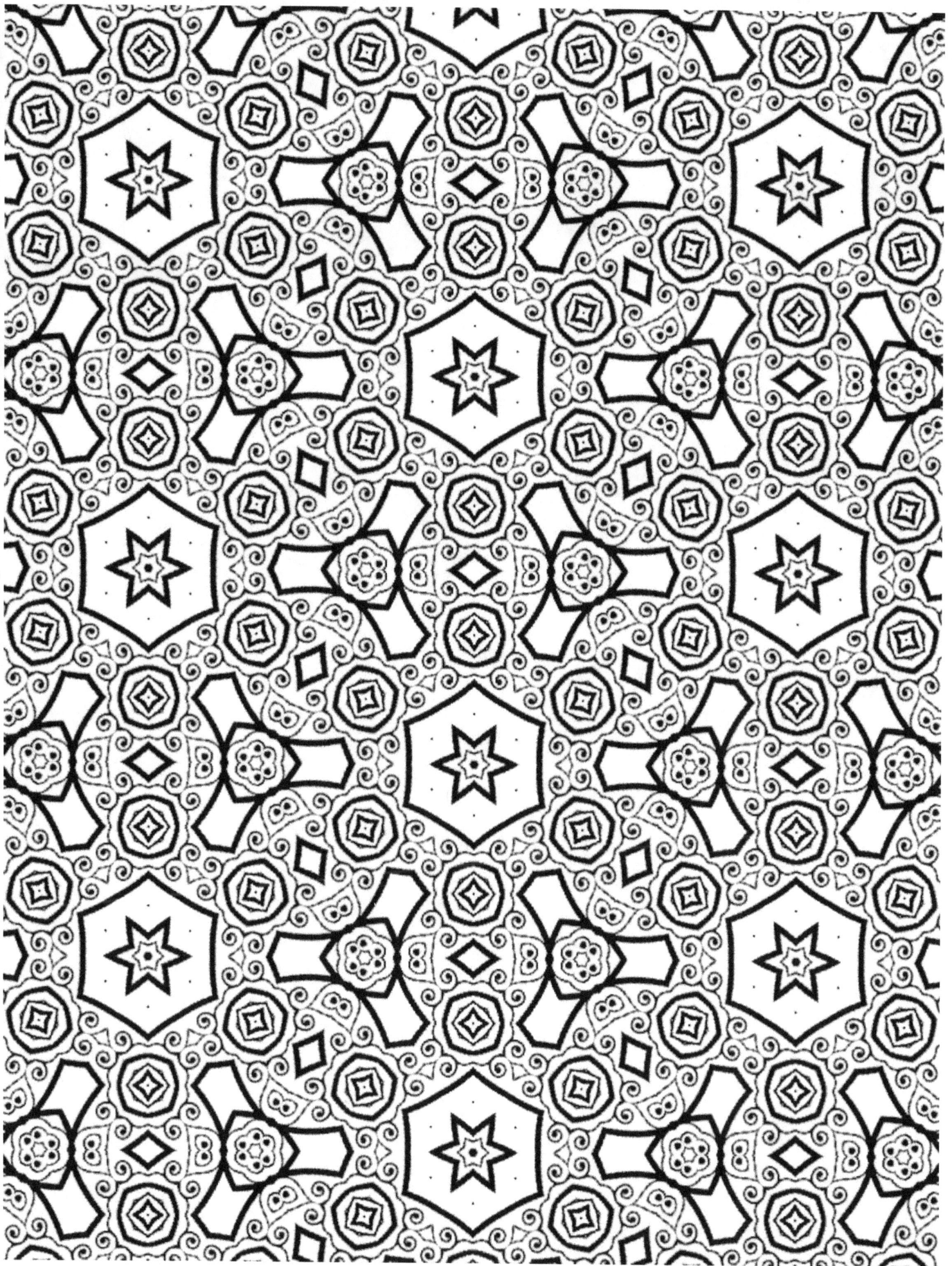

www.ingramcontent.com/pod-product-compliance
Lightning Source LLC
Chambersburg PA
CBHW080524030426
42337CB00023B/4621